I0460780

GET YOUR SH!T
TOGETHER 101

Get Your Sh!t Together 101

Kenn Edwards

First Printing, 2025

ISBN (paperback) 979-8-9887782-7-1

www.runewalker.com

Kenn Edwards
PO Box 188
Stockton, Utah
84071
USA

Contents

1

Preface

Thank you for buying and reading this publication. I wrote it because I see a need for a stripped-down, introductory guide to beginning your journey of personal and/or spiritual development. I have worked with so many folks, and the basics in the book are something we all need to help make our lives better and happier. The book is also a good place to start when you want to develop your psychic abilities, whether as a healer, reader, or spirit worker.

I hope you use this book. Write in it. Mark it up. Highlight ideas that inspire you. Keep track of your experiences so that you can trust yourself by seeing your track record and patterns.

Do this work for you! Do this for your current and future relationships (family, friends, colleagues, lovers). Create habits of Centering, Grounding, Shielding, and Cleansing. These will increase the quality of your life. However, be aware that they will shift your life. They will make you see things and people as they are. You may lose people from your life; this may hurt initially but will bring you peace in the long run.

2

Introduction

No one is beyond a 101-level book. No, not even you. And sure as hell not me. We fall back to the basics when faced with stressful or new situations. What are your basics? What are your foundations?

I have worked with thousands of people over my lifetime, specifically in a spiritual context, for the past two decades. Unfortunately, I have repeatedly seen the consequences of a lack of solid basics. This book contains foundational exercises and some tips and tricks.

Getting our sh!t together can be tricky in this fast-paced society. When I say "Get Your Sh!t Together," what do you think of? I think of those times in the day when I feel overwhelmed and like things are really out of my control. I seem to be at the mercy of everyone and everything else. These situations can become more frequent over time or have already for you. This book aims to give you some basics to combat these moments and their increased frequency.

Let's define or describe having your sh!t together. But first, what does it mean to you? Take a minute to list out some ideas. No, seriously, stop reading and do it.

According to Merriam-Webster.com, the definition is:

> : to begin to proceed in an effective way: to become prepared, organized, etc.

The word "effective" stands out to me in this definition and needs to be clarified. The same source, Merriam-Webster.com, states that one meaning of effective is:

: ready for service or action

I enjoy researching the origins and definitions of words. I believe it is essential to know what one's words mean. Sometimes, we use words with multiple meanings, or the generally agreed-upon meaning is not our understanding. In these ways, we may be misrepresenting our intentions.

In this book, our goal is to be able to interact with life experiences while maintaining an awareness of our own needs and desires by minimizing the influences around us.

The information and exercises in this book will help achieve this goal.

This book will be to the point. So, let's get started.

3

Foundations

Buildings have foundations to protect their structural integrity from aging and outside factors. Foundations consist of more than concrete. They also include the necessary materials and how they will be used, obtained, and cared for. Using this imagery, one can envision a small shed or structure and extract essential features.

Essential features in this structure could include: wood, concrete, nails, plans, screws, hammer, level, shingles, and hinges.

You have foundations. You may not be aware of these structures that hold you up or keep you in good repair. Some of these foundations are weak or cracked. For many of us, these foundations were given to us by a religion or society in which we grew up. In my interactions with clients, I have seen that the later structures fail us when our faith wavers or we leave that group altogether. Of course, this is not the only reason, but it is a major one.

In this book, we are strictly dealing with information and practices to help you Get Your Sh!t Together. In the following pages, you will find foundational practices that can help you. Use them all. Use some of them. There is no requisite or expectation.

wood	connections
concrete	cycles
nails	centering
plans	grounding
screws	shielding
hammer	hygiene
level	trust
shingles	belief system
hinges	follow through
window	implementation
door handle	patience

Follow Through Questions

1. What foundational practices do you currently have that support you?
2. What foundational practices have you tried to implement in the past that did not support you?
3. Why did these not work?
4. What foundational practices are needed to accomplish your current goals and desires?
5. What has stopped you from fully embracing and implementing these practices?

4

Connection

Connection is the awareness that two or more things are related. There are many different types of connections, and this chapter discusses three main categories.

Why is this the first foundation chapter? Why is understanding connection meaningful? In this ever-evolving and fast-paced Western civilization, there is a focus on individual achievement. While this would not be a negative trait, it is vital to recognize a loss of supportive relationships. Even more notable is the lack of relationship with the local environments in which we live. Connection is a key piece of understanding.

PHYSICAL CONNECTION

This one should be easy to grasp. Physical connection is when the physically manifested form of two or more things (persons, plants, animals, or any physically manifested item in our reality) come into physical contact.

Touch is an integral part of our interaction with the world. Through touch, we experience hot and cold, soft and hard. We experience our blood rush when our lips touch a romantic partner's. We experience the chewy texture and savor the garlic butter seasoning on the escargot.

Physical connection through contact can be a great tool when trying to develop awareness. For those of you building a spiritual practice, Psychometry is an excellent example of using a physical connection to access the other two connection types and practice your skills. For those building a personal practice, our ability to reach out and grasp things in our immediate vicinity allows us to manage our physical spaces.

Organization appears differently to everyone. Do you function better in a highly organized room, a clean room, or a disheveled room?

ENERGETIC CONNECTION

Energetic connection is imperceptible to the human eye (for most people). This will be the basic definition used here.

These connections act much like phone calls. Both parties can send and receive information via speech and hearing during a phone call. This visual represents what an energetic connection would look like if we could see it.

Energetic connections happen all the time. Have you ever been in a great conversation with a friend, and things are flowing so well that you finish each other's sentences? This is an excellent example. When I owned Blue Antler, a spiritual and metaphysical shop, I encouraged patrons searching for a crystal or stone to pick them up and feel them. This physical touch leads to what one could describe as a spark. It's that moment when a connection is felt more profound than physical touch. The feeling can be likened to when we become inspired. This energetic connection often makes us feel alive. This is one of the easiest to point out. There are also energetic connections that encourage us to run the other way.

SPIRITUAL CONNECTION

The main difference between energetic and spiritual connections is that a spiritual connection comes through or from source, a deity, or the divine. I would say that all spiritual connections are energetic, but not all energetic connections are spiritual. This is my point of view. Some have the exact opposite. For example, if your belief system sees all things as one and that one is divine, then all connections are spiritual. Which definition feels right for you?

GETTING MY SH!T TOGETHER

Everything is connected. At the beginning of my spiritual development, I found some connections that may or may not have meaning. However, just because all things are connected doesn't mean that there is meaning when we experience two or more things that seem related. This gets a bit confusing, right? Correlation does not equal causation.

I have a metaphorical box. This box is full of puzzle pieces. The pieces all belong to a giant puzzle. When assembling puzzles we purchase at a store, we usually have the box to show us what the final picture looks like. This is NOT the case with my spiritual journey.

I pick up these metaphorical puzzle pieces in the form of slight feelings, images, or other things pointed out to me by my spirit guides, ancestors, or instinct. Sometimes, if I'm lucky, I even get two that fit together. Understanding connections and what connections feel like helps us recognize when we are receiving guidance and when we have two puzzle pieces that share a relationship and, therefore, fit together.

In building my practice and myself, connection is not merely building my network of friends, colleagues, and clients. It is pivotal in my growth. Understanding my needs and meeting them is all about connections, especially when I make the connection between eating and being comforted. Becoming aware of these small connections and their origins is part of learning to navigate oneself and putting together a spiritual or non-spiritual practice that meets our needs.

Follow Through Questions

1. What is your definition of connection?
2. What people do you feel connected to and why?
3. What seemingly inanimate objects do you have a connection with and why?
4. What experiences have you had that are synchronicities?
5. What experiences have you had that you thought were synchronicities and weren't?
6. What was the difference between the experiences in the last two questions?
7. Which connections mean the most to you?
8. Which connections are essential for your survival?
9. What are some of your needs that aren't met?
10. What connections need to be made or acknowledged that would meet those needs?

5

Cycles

In today's modern Western societies, many of us think that the growth cycle of food consists of going to the grocery store, taking food from the shelf, taking it home, and eating it. When we need more, we go back to the grocery store; magically, there is more on the shelf. I know that is potentially an overly dramatic statement, but the roots of the thought originate in the tree of truth! Intertwined with this problematic concept of food's origins is the problem of impatience and "I want it now, Daddy!"

It is necessary to discuss the concept of cycles.

Let's talk about growing a food or herb garden. One can look at the phases of life for the soil and plants as planting, growing, harvesting, and resting. It is essential to know when each of these begins and ends. Where I live, most plants are planted outside toward the end of May. These plants then need to be fed and watered in the appropriate amounts. Weeds must be removed to make nutrients and sunshine available for the plants. When it is time, usually weeks or months later, you can harvest the food from the plant. At the end of the growing season, steps are taken to ensure the soil is good for the next growing season. And then the ground rests for a period of time.

If we consider being a surgeon, does a doctor read about or watch a video online and immediately go into surgery to repair the heart muscle? No. The process is key. The processing of information and experience is key! Practice is key! Patience is key! It's not even patience; it's honoring and accepting the cycle of life.

The diversity of humanity dictates a diversity in personal cycles. And those cycles vary depending on the cycles of the earth and universe. For instance, I have become aware that the closer I get to a birthday, the less energy I have. It is optimal for me to get plenty of rest and not over-schedule during this time. Another quick acknowledgment is that the full moon does not let me sleep well. Therefore, I try not to schedule appointments too early on days around the full moon.

Many times with myself and clients, I have used the following exercise to gain perspective:

Picture a glacier. You've seen one in books, videos, or perhaps in person. If you haven't, please take a moment to look one up to have a good image in your mind and awareness. Imagine yourself standing on a glacier. You are standing in the middle of an ice field many times larger than a football field stretching in all directions. In the very far distance, you see the ocean. On the other three sides are towering mountain ridges, sharp from thousands of years of carving.

The only movement you feel is the wind on your face and in your hair. The movement passing your ear makes a soft whistle. You feel entirely still except for this wind. The glacier below you feels solid and sure, although it isn't. The cracks and crevices aren't always visible. There are perhaps rivers of glacial water running through and under the glacier. The glacier's edges are scouring the hard stone of the earth, moving almost imperceptibly. Now, you can imagine the movement and action happening in the glacier, which seems to be at a standstill.

Sometimes, we feel like nothing is happening, but that's false. This resting period is necessary for integrating knowledge, wisdom, and practice. We all have cycles. Do you ever wonder why you are not harvesting what you desire? Is it because you are planting it in the wrong season or soil?

Follow Through Questions

1. What is your natural rhythm?
2. Does your creative cycle follow the moon's cycles?
3. What effect does the sun have on you?
4. What effect does the moon have on you?
5. How do you feel during each season (Winter, Spring, Summer, Fall)?
6. Why do you resist rest?
7. Where in your life are you planting in barren fields expecting growth?
8. Where have you planted seeds yet not taken care of or harvested the results?

6

Centering

One key to successful spiritual or emotional development is the ability to center ourselves. Centering is achieving a state of alignment, which creates a calm attitude, body, and emotional state.

Centering, Grounding, and Meditation may have similar goals depending on their definitions. Therefore, you can use one or all. However, in this book, I have structured them as components in a larger structure. Centering and Grounding are to calm the body, and Meditation is to calm the mind.

Centering results in the ability to distinguish one's life force and energy from that of others. The energy of others can affect us in both negative and positive ways. No matter the impact, our goal is to hear our voices and desires unaffected by the will of others.

Imagine a hectic day. The list of tasks and appointments is longer than the day itself. You are going a hundred miles per hour, and the whirlwind of to-do items surrounding you is even faster. That's a lot to balance, and your energy is spinning around you. During times like this, you may need to pause and regroup, gather your thoughts and ideas, and breathe. That is Centering.

The idea is to bring all those things spinning around you either back into you, if they are yours, or send them back to where they came from. Bringing everything to a standstill will help you to focus on the next task before you and not be distracted. This aids our ability to be present in each moment, interaction, and decision.

During Centering practice, you may find that you have an excess of or require more energy. This is where Grounding comes in, which is why it is the next section. Let's look at a fundamental way to center yourself.

Centering

1. Find a calm place with silence, or use headphones to remove distracting sounds. This will become irrelevant as you grow more capable of eliminating sounds from your awareness. If you're at work, this may be a janitorial closet. If at home with a house full of rambunctious kids and spouses, this may be the laundry room — no one wants to help with that chore.
2. Find a comfortable seated position (lying down works well, but you may end up taking a nap instead).
3. Close your eyes and place your hand on your lower abdomen.
4. As you inhale, push your hand outward by expanding your lower abdomen. The goal is to breathe deeply and relax your shoulders and neck, which tend to be tense as you raise and lower your shoulders in rushed breathing.
5. Try the four-fold breath pattern. Some practitioners find it easy to envision drawing a box during this. Begin by inhaling for four counts. Hold that breath for four counts. Exhale for four counts. Hold that for four counts. Repeat.

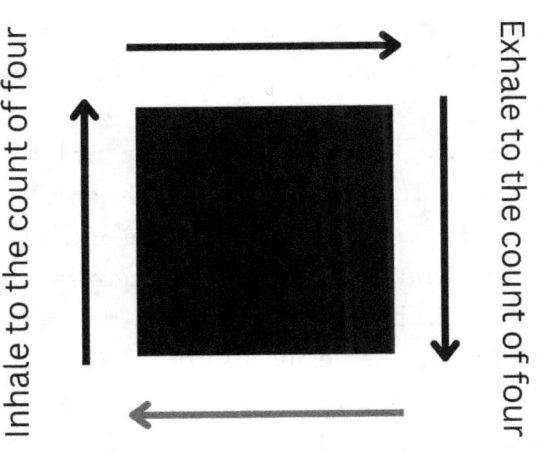

This practice does not have a specific time allotment. I have experienced it for as little as one minute with success. If your mind wanders away and begins thinking about your to-do list, gently guide yourself back to focusing on your breath. It can help to make your to-do list before you sit down to center yourself. This gives you confidence that nothing will be forgotten. And don't worry about doing it too much, it's impossible.

A driving factor and influence in my life is the Northern Traditions of Pre-Christian Europe. The Runes are central to this. One of the Runes that I love for centering is Isa. Isa means ice. I begin with the breathing technique listed above. As my breathing settles in, I softly speak the word Isa. I visualize a needle-thin icicle entering the top of my head. It slowly moves down the center of my body until it exits my perineum. The icicle continues to lower between my legs to the floor; my vision is of me standing, even if I'm sitting.

Once the icicle has passed through the center, I imagine it expanding and growing thicker as

I inhale and exhale. I continue until the icicle encompasses my body. As it develops, I see it freezing in place, the things whirling around me, stopping their motion and allowing me to handle them when ready.

This technique can be beneficial when people and their emotions, which can act like wrecking balls of energy, are whirling around you. You are in control of your physical space and energy.

ISA

Follow Through Questions

1. Have you ever felt centered?
2. What did feeling centered feel like?
3. What were your capabilities while centered?
4. Have you ever felt very messy and unfocused?
5. What were your capabilities when you felt that way?
6. What was your experience trying the fourfold breathing technique?
7. What was challenging?
8. What was easy?
9. After a week of doing this practice daily, did you experience any differences in your behavior? If so, what were they?

7

Grounding

Are you an electrician? I am not an electrician. And it is necessary to delve into that for just a moment. Grounding is called grounding for a reason.

A ground wire is a safety measure that directs excess electricity into the ground. Excess electricity can damage equipment or even start a fire if there is no outlet or way to escape.

Grounding is the act of focusing the excess energy from our systems (physical, mental, emotional, energetic, spiritual) and transferring that to the ground while simultaneously bringing up energy from the earth (or another source) to heal, inspire, create, etc. The last part adds to the basic concept of electricity shared above.

The image used for Grounding is often a tree's taproot descending deep into the earth. We send down this taproot after Centering (see previous section). When you have reached a comfortable depth, send down the excess energy you have built up. After you feel it moving, begin pulling up the healing powers from the earth to replenish and give sustenance. This is a good visualization technique for Grounding. Visualizing and feeling may be difficult initially, but both will be strengthened and come more easily to you with practice.

A Taproot is the primary root of the system growing vertically downward. Its principal function is to provide deep anchorage and help absorb nutrients and water from the soil.

Why is it good to ground? What are the benefits?

- Rid yourself of excess energy that may be causing distraction, anxiety, depression, or restless sleep
- Connect with the earth and receive energy
- Calmness
- Less stress on all systems
- More control over our output/words/intentions

_____
_____
_____
_____
_____
_____
_____
_____
_____
_____
_____
_____
_____
_____

Grounding

1. As you continue breathing (four-fold or otherwise), feel your spine extend into the ground below you.
2. Feel the top of your spine extend up toward the sky.
3. Within the spine are two channels, one going down and one going up. Picture a full circle being made by connecting to the earth below and the sky.
4. When you have established the flow of this cycle through you and can feel it solidly, begin to pool all the excess energy you feel in your body, mind, and spirit systems at the center of your body around the belly button.
5. When complete, release the energy into the down channel into the earth.
6. Continue to feel the complete cycle and movement of energy through you.

This practice can also help other people experiencing distress, but it has to be utilized correctly and account for the surroundings. You can ground into different mediums, not just Earth. Once, I was on a plane that was experiencing terrible turbulence. We flew the very short distance from Salt Lake City, Utah, to Denver, Colorado. I was seated next to an energy healer friend of mine. This friend just happened to be afraid of flying and hated small spaces.

After trying to help alleviate some of their anxiety, I realized that I was experiencing them trying to ground their excess energy. Great idea! Until I realized that they were trying to ground into the earth. After my lightbulb moment, I asked if they were Grounding, and they replied yes.

At this point, what did I have to lose? I joked that they would cause the plane to crash with the amount of power they had been trying to force to the ground. I laughed, and so did they. We switched up the tactics, and they connected to the element of air instead. It looked and worked the same as the steps described above. It worked! My friend felt better. And I'm not making this shit up: The turbulence significantly lessened.

Grounding into the four elements of Earth, Air, Fire, or Water is possible and takes some practice. We all have one that feels natural and is our most substantial ground. Once you have a feel for it with Earth, try the others. If Earth feels impossible after weeks of practice, try another one you feel more connected to.

Follow Through Questions

1. When would Grounding be an appropriate exercise for you in daily life?
2. What challenges have you had Grounding previously?
3. How can you overcome those challenges?
4. When you achieved feeling grounded, what did it feel like?
5. Are there times when you have naturally felt grounded?
6. What are the results of Grounding in the morning and before bed?

8

Shielding

We all know what a windshield is, right? The piece of glass preventing you from getting bugs in your teeth and your nicely coiffed hair from being a tangled mess. It also prevents you from getting wet, dusty, and cold when the elements are less than friendly to our fragile human bodies. A personal energetic shield works similarly, except it provides a barrier that can prevent you from the intrusive and sloppy energy of other beings, including humans.

Complete the steps to Center and Ground as listed in the previous sections, then do the following:

Shielding

1. Begin to separate a small amount of the energy flowing through you and focus it into a small sphere near your belly button.
2. Focus on continuing to feed this sphere and watch it grow. The sphere will encapsulate your physical and energetic bodies.
3. Stop the growth when the sphere has expanded to approximately a foot above your head and below your feet. Allow the energy to flow through the sphere just as it does through your body: It flows from the earth into you and out to the sky, and the opposite happens simultaneously.
4. Inhale and exhale a few times.
5. On the next inhale, feel the sphere move closer to you and begin to match the shape of your body. As the sphere condenses, it becomes more robust and more impenetrable.
6. Feel the sphere settle into its new shape on the exhale.
7. You can try this several times until the energy sphere is the same shape as your body but about six inches from the edges of your physical form.

Shielding is a critical skill to develop. I need you to hear this one thing: You do not have to be available to people 24/7. It is not mean or abusive to have boundaries. It is not selfish to have boundaries. It is the best way to serve your family and community. Be sovereign. Have edges and boundaries that are healthy and keep you from being overwhelmed.

This is necessary if you are also trying to develop your psychic abilities. As a reader, healer, and human being, I must distinguish my aches, pains, and emotions from those of the person I am helping. This is crucial to your success but will only be accomplished after some time. It takes time and practice.

You Do NOT Need to be available to people 24/7

GETTING MY SH!T TOGETHER

One day, many years ago, I visited a metaphysical store, not looking for anything specific, just browsing. I also love to experience other people's gifts, watching how they work and the energy flows through them. I am always on the lookout for readers I feel drawn to.

I used to cruise through life without shields. I blissfully wandered along, naively thinking that I was safe. I thought no one wanted to hurt others, and I was protected. I learned quickly that shields are a good practice. Although I was not harmed, I was shaken.

The month before visiting this metaphysical store, I had been doing a lot of journey work, traveling here and there astrally. I had taken a big trip with the guidance of a spirit worker to visit the council of light in the cosmos. While I won't get into it in this book, those folks are shady as fuck. I was still processing that and had some sleep troubles and anxiety. So, this was on my mind.

The store employee, who happened to be a spirit worker, was chatting with me like a regular interaction. They then asked if I was tired. I replied yes and said that I had been busy lately. They then responded that doing so much traveling will do that to a person. Without thinking, I agreed, and then it hit me like a ton of bricks. They were reading me and "tapping in" to me. I felt violated. That was none of their business.

This is precisely why I ask people for permission to read them before beginning. I do not believe that they had malicious intent. It just freaked me out that they could see everything. No one needs to know that much about anyone else. I only went into that place again with full shields. And on the other end of the spectrum, just a thought: If you're shielding and holding your shit together, you won't be broadcasting or spraying your energy vomit all over other people.

Follow Through Questions

1. Shield yourself before going into the grocery store. How did this change your experience?
2. Shield yourself from someone you constantly feel drained after speaking to. Did this change your energy level? What did you feel happened during your time together?
3. What visualization worked best when sustaining the shield?
4. What things or people have you noticed immediately took down that shield?
5. Who causes your shield to rise unconsciously?
6. Who do you need better boundaries with?

9

Meditation

I know! I know! You're thinking, "I can't meditate!" or "I've tried to meditate, and it doesn't work!" You may even think, "I don't have time to meditate." Can you spare one to five minutes per day? That's all you need to start this.

Ideally, we seek an intentional state of calm and awareness through focus. In the chapter on Centering, I stated that Centering, Grounding, and Meditating all have similar goals. Meditation seeks to calm and focus the mind.

There are many ways to accomplish this. Moving meditation can provide just as much calm and awareness as still meditation. Examples of moving meditation are hiking, riding a bike or motorcycle, gardening, painting, or martial arts. Don't box yourself in. You have felt the quiet of reaching a meditative state. What were you doing? Start there.

The word "meditate" can be associated with a lot of pressure. Many modern images create expectations that can be challenging to meet in our constant-movement Western culture. So, maybe we need some different words that don't carry this weight.

- Contemplation
- Thinking
- Pondering
- Reflection
- Prayer
- Study
- Concentration

These words seem way more doable. They're not so scary. They are not insurmountable. So, what now? Choose one of the above words, and use this word instead of Meditation when you speak about calming your mind and narrowing your focus.

As you become more comfortable with this, you can choose another word from the list that is more appropriate for the focus. For example, if you intend to send love and care to someone or something, you may use the word "prayer."

It could be an oversimplification, but Meditation is just training your mind to stay focused on one topic. The imagery in the Centering chapter about a hectic day can be applied to the thoughts that can bombard your mind. Take a moment to go back and read that section again, except this time, think about the whirlwind being your thoughts.

Quick Tip

Write down the list of things you need to do after your contemplation time on a separate piece of paper or on your phone. This can help eliminate these distractions and worry that you will forget them.

Follow Through Questions

1. What do you find hard about meditating?
2. Can you write that list down and throw it away?
3. Which word did you immediately choose to replace meditation?
4. What other ways can you meditate?
5. Does your choice of meditation depend on the time of day?
6. What have you already been doing that allows you to reach a state of calm and awareness?

10

Hygiene

Personal cleanliness is vital to our health and for creating and maintaining healthy relationships. Energetic hygiene is no different. The best example is the kitchen sink sponge.

You can already imagine the scent of the old sponge, can't you? It has been sitting in the water and getting very odorous. It wasn't always brown and stinky. It was once clean and free from food particles and bacteria. I know you think it should be thrown out and another purchased. What if this is the only sponge you're allowed? One sponge for your whole life. If you take care of that sponge, it will last a long time. The same thing happens with us. This book's Center, Ground, and Shield exercises will significantly reduce sluggish and stinky energy build-up.

Let's take a look at some possible effects of poor spiritual hygiene:

- Lack of energy
- Lack of focus
- Lack of feeling connected
- Increase in physical aches and pains
- Irritable
- Lack of empathy
- Lack of access to spiritual gifts

Of course, the effects of good spiritual hygiene would be the opposite of those things.

In addition to keeping ourselves clean, we should be aware of those around us who are slingers of their spiritual filth. You may have already imagined that monkey at the zoo that throws its feces at the cute little kids passing by.

Getting slimed by other people is an unpleasant experience; this can happen throughout our day.

Imagine a time when you were grumpy with the cashier at the grocery store who did nothing to you. You were most likely very frustrated with another situation or irritated with the lines and had somewhere to be. You slimed the poor cashier. We've all done it. You will do it less now because you are aware and have the tools to prevent it.

But what do you do when you get slimed? Or, the other monkeys in this circus throw their poo at you? You can add one of the following to your Center, Ground, and Shield process or use it separately when you need quick cleansing.

1. Keep a small spray bottle of cleansing essential oils, herbs, and stones, and spray yourself with it.
2. When you have created your Shield, divert some of the incoming energy to create a shower of cleansing energy.
3. Masturbate. This is a great way to build up and focus any energy, whether intentions/desires or excess and disperse it.
4. Shower. I mean, literally. Get in the shower and wash yourself.

GETTING MY SH!T TOGETHER

No one ever thinks they're the problem. It's always someone else. For instance, I once lived with two other people in a shared home. One of them is a spirit worker and very energy-sensitive. I am sometimes blissfully unaware that the bubble containing my energy is the size of a hot air balloon. When this happens, even if I am in a great mood, they become affected by my whirling energy. Their reaction to the whirling energy is not favorable. It unsettles the calm energy they prefer for their home space. I do not intentionally mean harm. It took me years to figure this out.

Unfortunately, I also take up the same amount of space when frustrated and angry. This sent my housemate over the edge. I used to think it was their fault that they were affected so much; they should shield themselves from my energy. What an asshole I was! I am responsible for my energy. You are responsible for yours. In my situation, I had agreed to live with two housemates and share space. To live honorably in this situation is to be respectful and cognizant of my energy's impact on the home and others living there.

The same could be said for the workplace as well. I used to work with someone who could change the complete mood of the place and everyone in it just by walking through the door. We would all say hi as they came in, and if they ignored the salutation, we knew we were in for a rough day. In addition, I think they fed off the misery and uneasiness they caused. Not cool and a total dick move! Don't be a dick! Keep yourself energetically clean!

Follow Through Questions

1. Which of the practices worked for you?
2. Have you been able to better recognize people with bad hygiene?
3. Have you been more aware of when your energy gets dirty and needs a good scrubbing?
4. How does the cleanliness of your physical space affect you?
5. How does the cleanliness of your physical space affect you after doing this program for three weeks?
6. In your research, what other hygiene practices have you found that you would like to try?

11

Trust Your Gut & Intuition

This one takes time, practice, and awareness. It also requires solid practice of everything discussed thus far in this book. You must be able to neutralize the noise of everything around you to hear and know yourself. Suppose you are developing relationships with unseen guides or psychic abilities. In that case, you must also be open to interactions with things beyond your normal physical senses. This requires you to trust your gut to know what is true and what is a sock puppet of your mind.

Trust is built over time, my friends. One must be willing to express one's experiences and track the outcomes. This is a good way to see patterns and help determine what works and what doesn't. The more this is done, the more aware we are of the signs that we can trust what we are experiencing.

First, we must figure out how to communicate with our body. Once we have reached a calm state in our body and mind, we can ask what feeling the body makes when something aligns with us. I suggest paying attention to your lower abdomen or gut. Most of us can identify with the concept that our gut hurts when it is telling us something is wrong. That is easier to identify. It is not enough to know what is incorrect or out of alignment; the "no." We must know the "yes" as well. So, what does it feel like when something is right or in alignment with you?

This skill is essential for everyone. The following paragraphs are more for those who want to develop relationships with unseen energies.

One way to work with your spirit team on this development is to provide them with guidelines on communicating with you. Please do not hand them a dictionary and say, "Learn this." Start small. When discerning between a male or female spirit, ask that male spirits appear in your energy field on the left and female spirits appear on the right. Simplicity is your friend here.

Another idea is to ask your spirit team to step into your energy field and step out. This helps to train your awareness to sense someone/something as it gets close to you. It also helps you to distinguish between your energy and that of others. There are so many simple techniques, but remember, the key is to keep track of them to begin formulating a working guide and building trust in your ability.

Tip: Keep a tally of the times your intuition was correct. Each hash mark is a reminder. This is an incredibly powerful tool. You don't need to record the specifics; just that it worked.

Quick Tip

Keep a tally of the times your intuition was correct.
Each hash mark is a reminder. This is an incredibly powerful tool. You don't need to record the specifics, just that it worked.

GETTING MY SH!T TOGETHER

How could I possibly know that her dead mother's favorite flowers were gardenias? Although I smelled them, I don't know what they smell like.

What does this image of a giant tiger jumping over this woman's shoulder have to do with me?

How did I know that the explosive feeling in my head was the result of experiencing how this man died?

All of these situations actually happened; all of them. These were just a few of the thousands of impressions/messages I've received while working with clients. How did I know they were real? How could I trust them? Over the years, I've learned what it feels, smells, sounds, and tastes like when an experience comes from something outside my body. I now explain the difference between looking at a car in one of those old View-

Master toys and seeing it in person. There is a different feel to the texture of it. Knowing the difference has taken years of being engaged in the activity. One thing I wish I had done was keep a journal of these experiences. I could have put it all together quicker and seen the patterns. Instead, I went from experience to experience, keeping them isolated and not seeing the bigger picture. Keep a journal!

Follow Through Questions

1. What does your gut feel like when something is wrong?
2. What does your gut feel like when something is right?
3. Where are you experiencing a disconnect between what your gut knows is true and what your brain dictates as truth?

12

Belief Systems

I choose and have been allowed to work within the Northern Traditions of Pre-Christian Europe, sometimes identified by the terms Norse Pagan, Anglo-Saxon Pagan, or Heathen. For the first part of my life, I was a devout Mormon. I have found my place in the roots of the beliefs of my ancestors. My worldview is influenced and inspired by the ideas and concepts as we have had them passed down. This is problematic for someone who comes from such a structured belief system. I enjoy the challenges faced as a modern Heathen, inspired by the past and living in this contemporary time.

Let's be open here; many of us have been screwed up/over by the expectations we have placed on ourselves in the name of a religious belief system. Agreed? Most people immediately attach religion to the word spiritual and exclude both when it comes to daily interactions. I have adopted the term worldview to overcome the possible roadblocks here. A worldview is the approach one takes to interacting with the world. This can be guided and shaped by one's ethics and values derived from a belief system rooted in religion, spirituality, logic, or a combination thereof.

Religion is not a necessity when it comes to Spiritual Development. It can, however, be a beautiful backdrop and support system for you. It is truly up to you whether or not you base your practice within the context of any belief system. You choose. If people decide to find a belief system, they should begin by forming their code of ethics and then find a system that works well with it.

Some systems may already have practices similar to those in this book that fit contextually. Songs, stories, and rituals may be used so often that they have their own power. This can enhance the energy behind your intention, making centering, grounding, shielding, cleansing, etc., more effective.

Use caution when engaging in intense or dangerous shamanic-style practices. In our modern society, with our ever-growing distaste for religion, we have removed practices from their traditions, and hence, we have removed some of the potential safeguards. You can get jacked up and injured with some of these things. Please use common sense and caution when working with the otherworlds. Remember, the unseen beings don't always have your best interests in mind.

Follow Through Questions

1. What is your current perception of religion?
2. What baggage do you have from past religious experiences?
3. Do you desire a belief system to engage with?
4. What are the potential benefits of working within an existing belief system?
5. What are the pitfalls of working within an existing belief system?

13

Now, Get Your Sh!t Together

Throughout my life, I have worked with clients and friends who have experienced distress. Unfortunately, this happens repeatedly. Understanding how we handle distress is integral to change. I mentioned that our reactions are rooted in our most practiced behavior when we react to something. Now is the time to change that practiced behavior.

This book is the perfect size to keep as a reminder and tracker of your progress. The goal is to create exercises that help you get and keep your sh!t together. I have made a tracking system for a six-week program. I have also left spaces for you to add your favorite exercises that may not be included here.

Tracking Tips

Don't give up!
So you missed a day, move on.

Once you become skilled at
Centering, Grounding, and Shielding,
it only takes a few minutes.

Keep track of the experiences: what
went well and what didn't.

Research different ways to cleanse,
physically and energetically.

Track Your Progress

Week 1	Centering	Grounding	Shieldin
Sunday	☐	☐	☐
Monday	☐	☐	☐
Tuesday	☐	☐	☐
Wednesday	☐	☐	☐
Thursday	☐	☐	☐
Friday	☐	☐	☐
Saturday	☐	☐	☐

Record your thoughts and notes on what went well and what did not.

_____

_____

_____

_____

_____

_____

_____

_____

_____

_____

_____

_____

_____

Track Your Progress

Track all of your "wins" when it comes trusting your intuition/gut! You only need to make hash marks.

Track Your Progress

	Meditation	Cleansing
Week 6		
Sunday	☐	☐
Monday	☐	☐
Tuesday	☐	☐
Wednesday	☐	☐
Thursday	☐	☐
Friday	☐	☐
Saturday	☐	☐

**Record your thoughts and notes on what
went well and what did not.**

Track Your Progress

Week 3	Centering		Grounding		Shielding	
	am	pm	am	pm	am	pm
Sunday	☐	☐	☐	☐	☐	☐
Monday	☐	☐	☐	☐	☐	☐
Tuesday	☐	☐	☐	☐	☐	☐
Wednesday	☐	☐	☐	☐	☐	☐
Thursday	☐	☐	☐	☐	☐	☐
Friday	☐	☐	☐	☐	☐	☐
Saturday	☐	☐	☐	☐	☐	☐

Record your thoughts and notes on what went well and what did not.

Track Your Progress

Week 2	Centering		Grounding		Shielding	
	am	pm	am	pm	am	pm
Sunday	☐	☐	☐	☐	☐	☐
Monday	☐	☐	☐	☐	☐	☐
Tuesday	☐	☐	☐	☐	☐	☐
Wednesday	☐	☐	☐	☐	☐	☐
Thursday	☐	☐	☐	☐	☐	☐
Friday	☐	☐	☐	☐	☐	☐
Saturday	☐	☐	☐	☐	☐	☐

Record your thoughts and notes on what
went well and what did not.

_____
_____
_____
_____
_____
_____
_____
_____
_____
_____
_____

Track Your Progress

Meditation

Week 3

Sunday	☐
Monday	☐
Tuesday	☐
Wednesday	☐
Thursday	☐
Friday	☐
Saturday	☐

Record your thoughts and notes on what went well and what did not.

_____
_____
_____
_____
_____
_____
_____
_____
_____
_____
_____
_____
_____
_____

Track Your Progress

Week 4	Centering am	pm	Grounding am	pm	Shieldir am	pm
Sunday	☐	☐	☐	☐	☐	☐
Monday	☐	☐	☐	☐	☐	☐
Tuesday	☐	☐	☐	☐	☐	☐
Wednesday	☐	☐	☐	☐	☐	☐
Thursday	☐	☐	☐	☐	☐	☐
Friday	☐	☐	☐	☐	☐	☐
Saturday	☐	☐	☐	☐	☐	☐

Record your thoughts and notes on what went well and what did not.

_____
_____
_____
_____
_____
_____
_____
_____
_____
_____
_____
_____
_____
_____

Track Your Progress

	Meditation	Energetic Cleansing
Week 4		
Sunday	☐	☐
Monday	☐	☐
Tuesday	☐	☐
Wednesday	☐	☐
Thursday	☐	☐
Friday	☐	☐
Saturday	☐	☐

Record your thoughts and notes on what went well and what did not.

_____

_____
_____
_____
_____
_____
_____
_____
_____
_____
_____
_____
_____
_____
_____

Track Your Progress

Week 5

	Centering			Grounding			Shieldin[g]		
	am	mid	pm	am	mid	pm	am	mid	p[m]
Sunday	☐	☐	☐	☐	☐	☐	☐	☐	☐
Monday	☐	☐	☐	☐	☐	☐	☐	☐	☐
Tuesday	☐	☐	☐	☐	☐	☐	☐	☐	☐
Wednesday	☐	☐	☐	☐	☐	☐	☐	☐	☐
Thursday	☐	☐	☐	☐	☐	☐	☐	☐	☐
Friday	☐	☐	☐	☐	☐	☐	☐	☐	☐
Saturday	☐	☐	☐	☐	☐	☐	☐	☐	☐

Record your thoughts and notes on what went well and what did not.

_____
_____
_____
_____
_____
_____
_____
_____
_____
_____
_____
_____
_____

Track Your Progress

Meditation   Cleansing

Week 5

Sunday ☐ ☐
Monday ☐ ☐
Tuesday ☐ ☐
Wednesday ☐ ☐
Thursday ☐ ☐
Friday ☐ ☐
Saturday ☐ ☐

Record your thoughts and notes on what went well and what did not.

_____
_____
_____
_____
_____
_____
_____
_____
_____
_____
_____
_____
_____
_____

Track Your Progress

Week 6	Centering			Grounding			Shieldin		
	am	mid	pm	am	mid	pm	am	mid	p
Sunday	☐	☐	☐	☐	☐	☐	☐	☐	☐
Monday	☐	☐	☐	☐	☐	☐	☐	☐	☐
Tuesday	☐	☐	☐	☐	☐	☐	☐	☐	☐
Wednesday	☐	☐	☐	☐	☐	☐	☐	☐	☐
Thursday	☐	☐	☐	☐	☐	☐	☐	☐	☐
Friday	☐	☐	☐	☐	☐	☐	☐	☐	☐
Saturday	☐	☐	☐	☐	☐	☐	☐	☐	☐

Record your thoughts and notes on what went well and what did not.

_____

_____

_____

_____

_____

_____

_____

_____

_____

_____

_____

_____

Centering

1. Find a calm place with silence, or use headphones to remove distracting sounds. This will become irrelevant as you grow more capable of eliminating sounds from your awareness. If you're at work, this may be a janitorial closet. If at home with a house full of rambunctious kids and spouses, this may be the laundry room — no one wants to help with that chore.
2. Find a comfortable seated position (lying down works well, but you may end up taking a nap instead).
3. Close your eyes and place your hand on your lower abdomen.
4. As you inhale, push your hand outward by expanding your lower abdomen. The goal is to breathe deeply and relax your shoulders and neck, which tend to be tense as you raise and lower your shoulders in rushed breathing.
5. Try the four-fold breath pattern. Some practitioners find it easy to envision drawing a box during this. Begin by inhaling for four counts. Hold that breath for four counts. Exhale for four counts. Hold that for four counts. Repeat.

Grounding

1. As you continue breathing (four-fold or otherwise), feel your spine extend into the ground below you.
2. Feel the top of your spine extend up toward th sky.
3. Within the spine are two channels, one going down and one going up. Picture a full circle being made by connecting to the earth below and the sky.
4. When you have established the flow of this cycle through you and can feel it solidly, begin to pool all the excess energy you feel in your body, mind, and spirit systems at the center of your body around the belly button.
5. When complete, release the energy into the down channel into the earth.
6. Continue to feel the complete cycle and movement of energy through you.

Shielding

1. Begin to separate a small amount of the energy flowing through you and focus it into a small sphere near your belly button.
2. Focus on continuing to feed this sphere and watch it grow. The sphere will encapsulate your physical and energetic bodies.
3. Stop the growth when the sphere has expanded to approximately a foot above your head and below your feet. Allow the energy to flow through the sphere just as it does through your body: It flows from the earth into you and out to the sky, and the opposite happens simultaneously.
4. Inhale and exhale a few times.
5. On the next inhale, feel the sphere move closer to you and begin to match the shape of your body. As the sphere condenses, it becomes more robust and more impenetrable.
6. Feel the sphere settle into its new shape on the exhale.
7. You can try this several times until the energy sphere is the same shape as your body but about six inches from the edges of your physical form.